MYNYDD PARYS

SMahi
10/12/90.

MYNYDD PARYS

poems by
Gwyn Parry

photographs by
Steve Makin

SEREN BOOKS

SEREN BOOKS is the book imprint of
Poetry Wales Press Ltd
Andmar House, Tondu Road
Bridgend, Mid Glamorgan

British Library Cataloguing in Publication Data

Parry, Gwyn *1962-*
    Mynydd Parys.
    I. Title
    821.914

ISBN 1-85411-038-1

*The publisher acknowledges the financial support of the
Welsh Arts Council*

Typeset in 11 point Palatino by Megaron, Cardiff
Printed by The Alden Press, Oxford

Contents

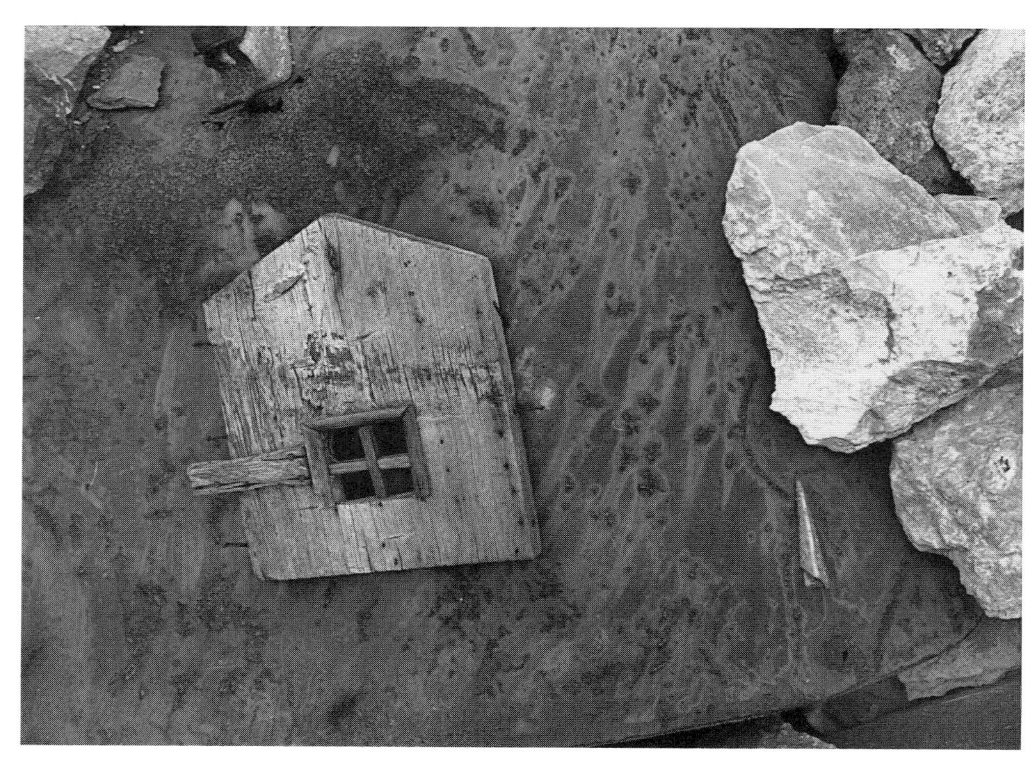

INTRODUCTION

On March 2nd, 1768, a huge deposit of copper was discovered on Mynydd Parys near Amlwch, on the north east coast of Anglesey. Mynydd Parys soon became one the largest copper mines in the world. It made Amlwch a boom town, local people left the working of the land for the higher wages in the mine: the work was hard, the conditions appalling.

The poet Dafydd Ddu o Eryri visited the mine in 1796, this was his impression:

> Och! hiraeth i'm carcharu, — arwy'myd,
> Eisieu maidd a llymru;
> Och, lwch pob parth, tarth bob tu,
> Ow! digon i'm dwbl dagu.

By the early 1880s most of the copper had been extracted, through the copper precipitation process continued into the early twentieth century.

I grew up with Mynydd Parys and its history. I became fascinated by its multi-coloured landscape, its silence and strange beauty; my fascination has grown with me over the years.

MYNYDD PARYS

On yellow bone rock
I establish my foothold.

I throw stones
into the fish-mouth hole,
no closer   I will fall.

I draw my finger
through the softness
of sulphur.

I handle rocks,
splendid in their colours
like tropical fish.

I know a way inside,
a shoulder-width hole,
I avoid its socket of black.

I climb to the glitter
of iron and zinc,
sit on a zebra-striped rock.

I watch the sun anoint
the tallest spoil-heap

watch it roll down the light
of the afternoon.

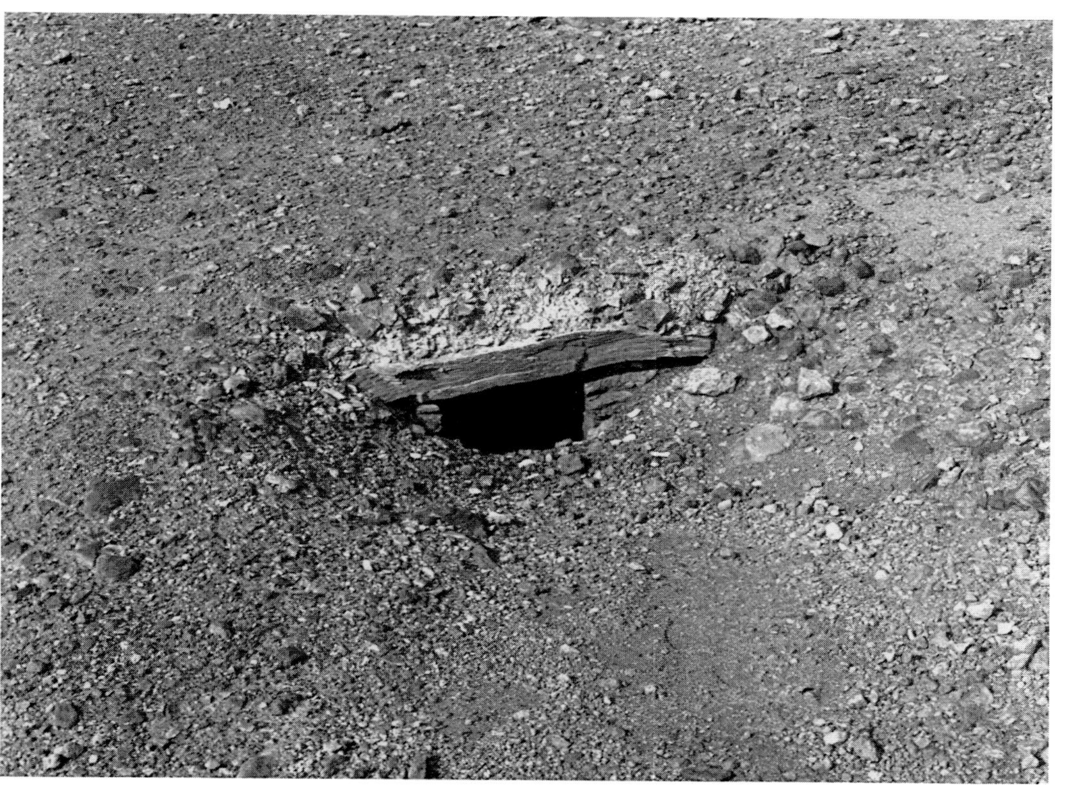

MYNYDD PARYS, JANUARY

A car-seat
lies gutless on the track

flesh-coloured paper snorts
in the piss-tinted lake.

After rain
the mountain shouts colour

the horizon fails to hold
the deep reds

the scratched blue skin
of stones.

No animals
on this metal carcass,

this place is all alone.

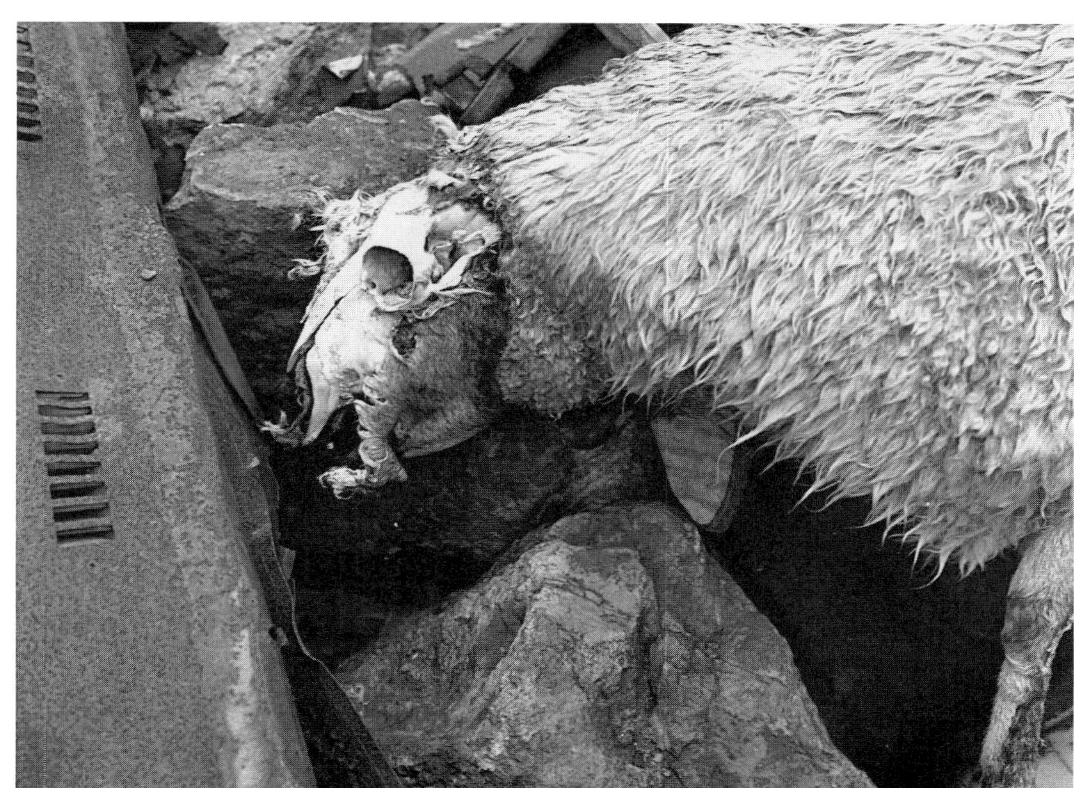

red stone
     sunset
weathered white
     wood
rib-cage shafts

ratchet voice
     raven
round knuckle
     mineral
bromide blood
     lakes

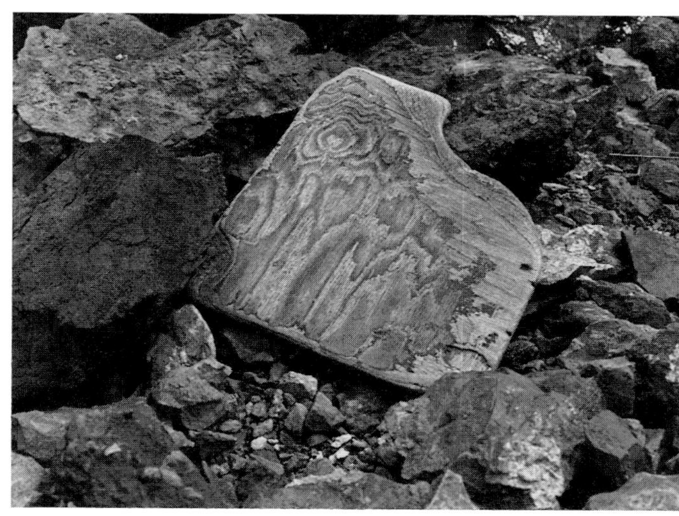

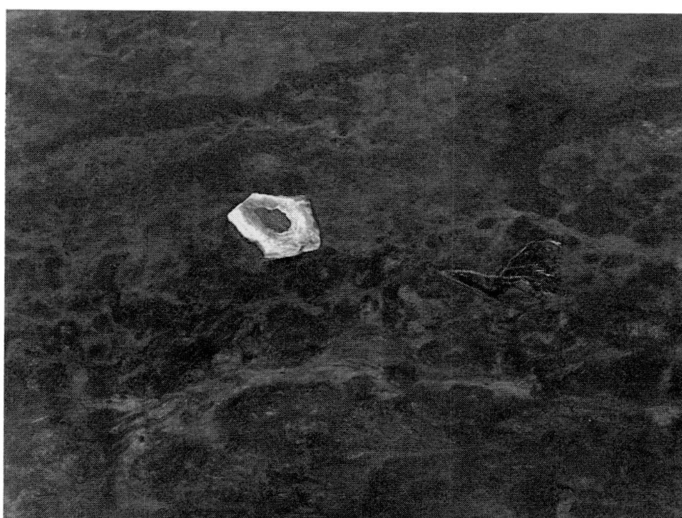

this place
    is blood
knocking
    metal
each heart rock
    taken
each vein
    burst

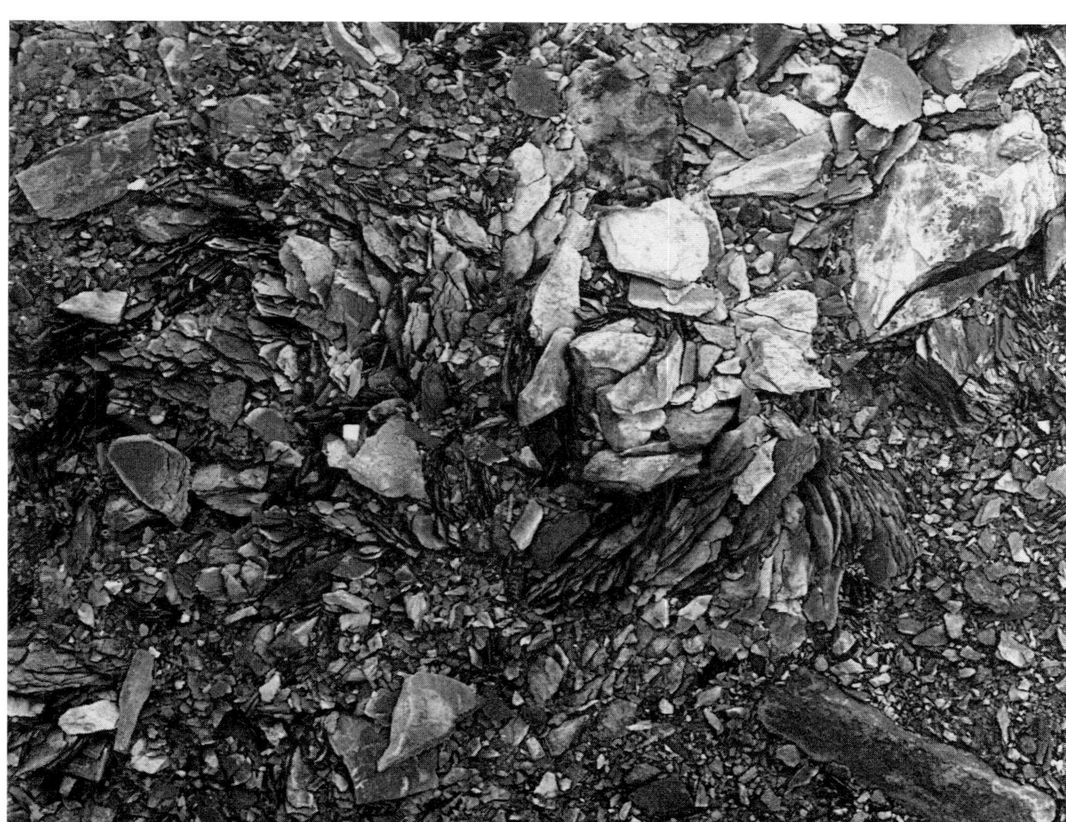

MURDER

She is naked,
cut dead pig.

Her blue thighs
fat under a tin-faced moon.

She lies all night,
stone on the mountain,
murdered by her lover.

Dumped amongst fridges,
radiators, lengths of rubber hose.

She has coloured the rocks
red and blue and red.

Her outline drawn
not in chalk
but ochre.

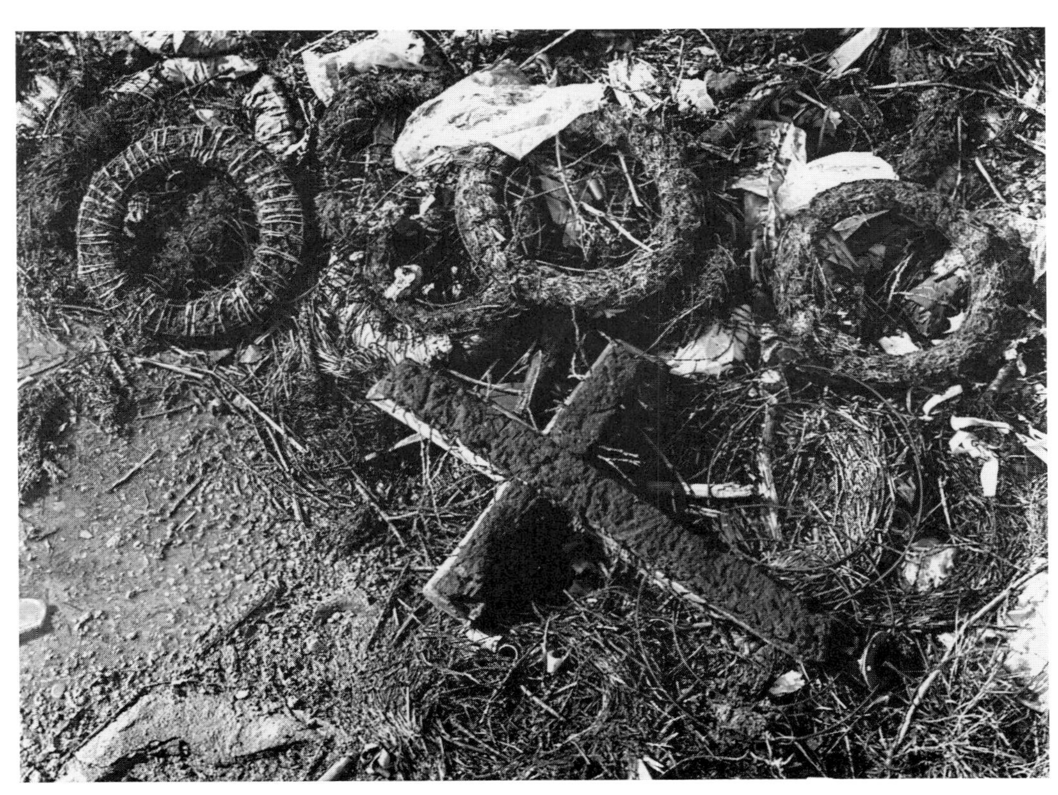

RAVEN

This is a place
where light has no claim,
where clouds gather
to rest for the night.

I have found the skull
smashed between rocks,
beak snapped from the head
like a bit of chalk.

I peel feathers off stone,
find bones
washed by the weather,
picked clean by the salt wind.

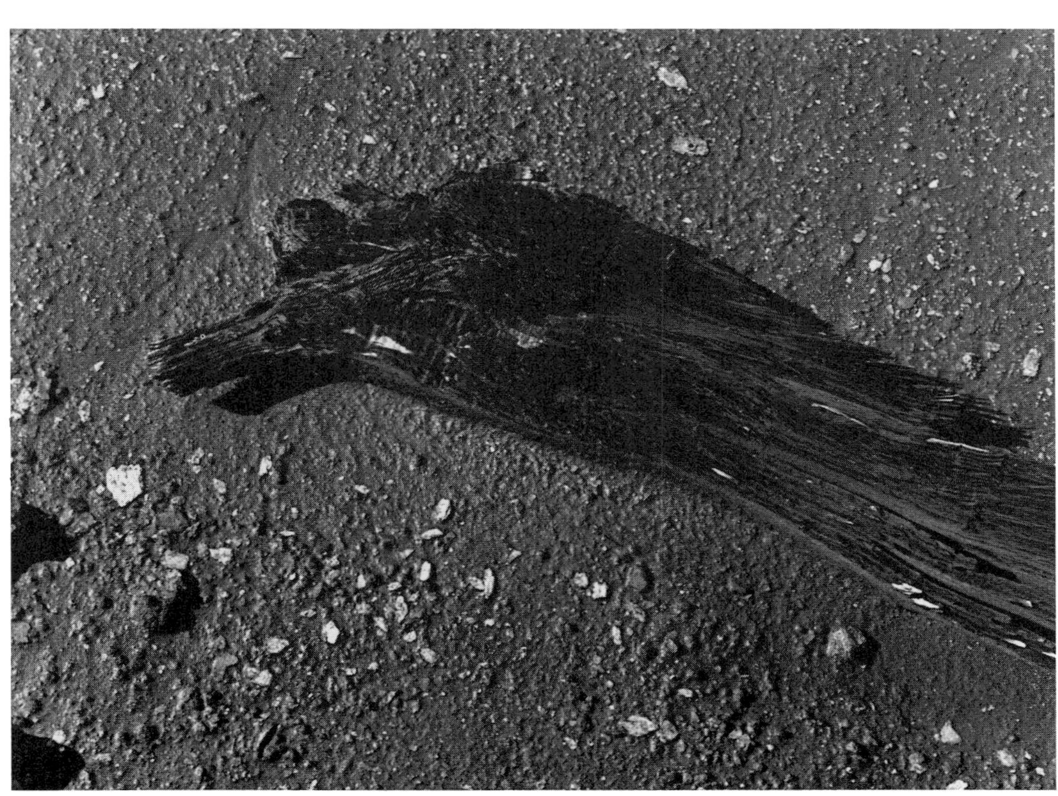

MEASURING

I perch on the open-cast,
hold the lake in my hand.

I measure the depth
in years.

Water slops in shafts,
open mouths wait
for every stone.

I throw a wheel
into the brown gut.

Slopes purple
to the water's edge

tyres hump-back
like poison eels.

Ravens measure eye
and wing beat

they watch my back
and where my shadow falls.

I measure land and sky
with wood and stones

the seconds they take to fall.

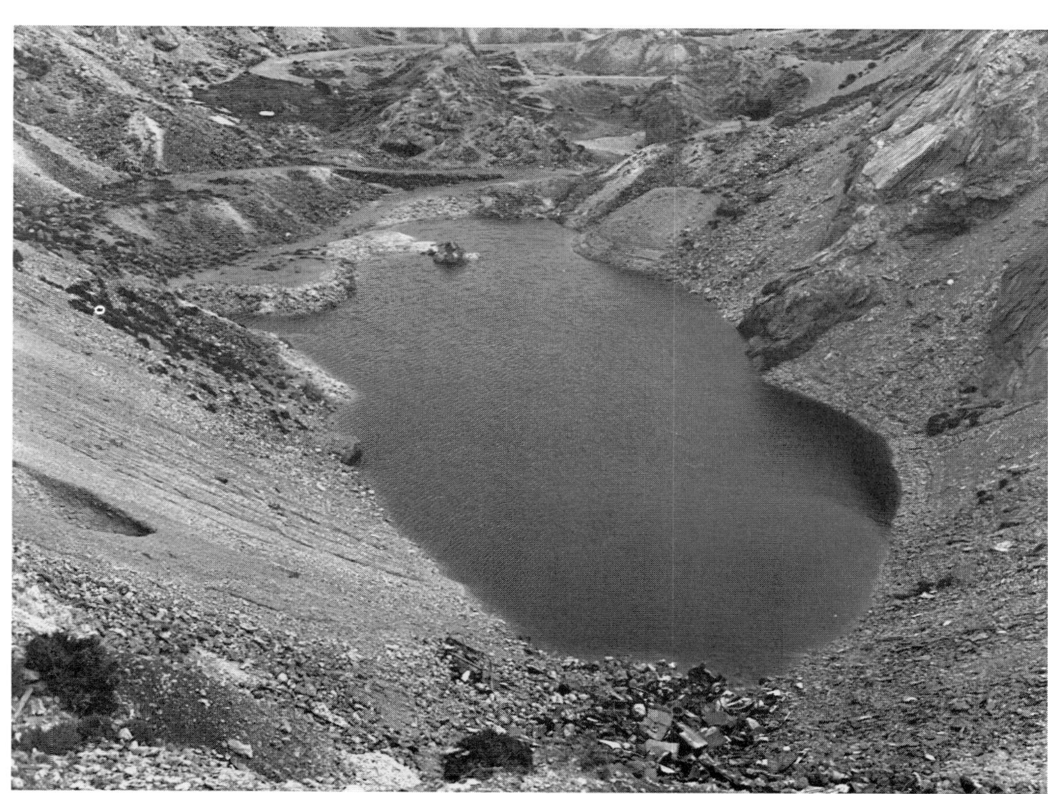

ECHO

I hit stone on rock
60 feet
above the open cast,
                       I knock
                       it knocks
echo of hand and hammer.

I break silence
with stone and rock,
I lie curved
on a high outcrop,
pierced
by the sun's warm spear.

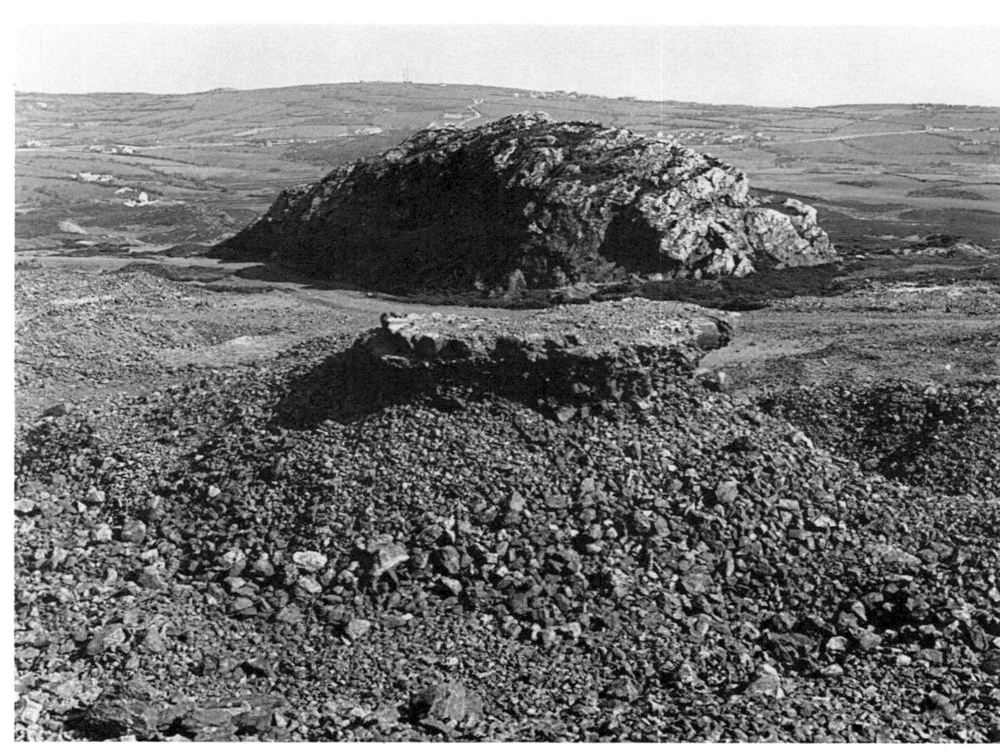

CAVE

The wind scrapes the mountain,
open sore.

Rocks are gutted
rotten fruit.

A mountain pulled-over
inside-out.

Entering the cave
darkness is shoulder-tight

my face a pin-point of light.

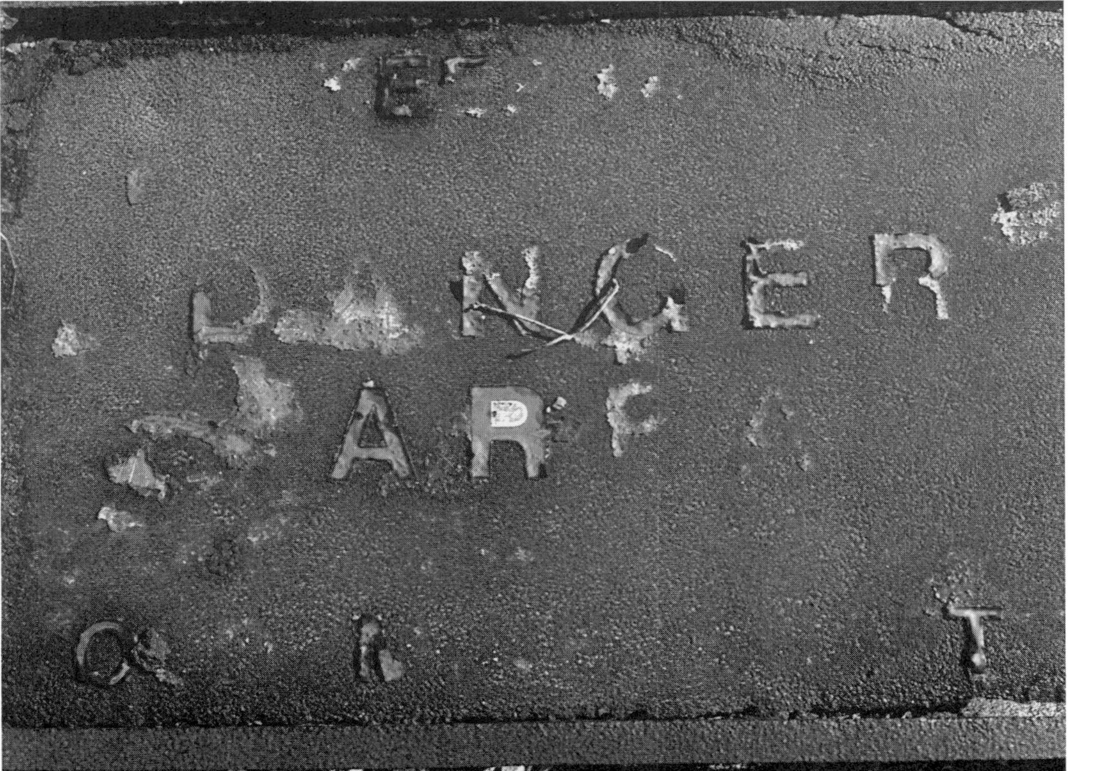
DANGER
AREA

OGOF

copper sulphate
    carreg las
wax beard bird shit
      on orange-green ledges,
water drips,
        kiss
            kiss
                kiss.
rocks fall
    through dark throats
of stone,
    noises gas-up
from a deep level.

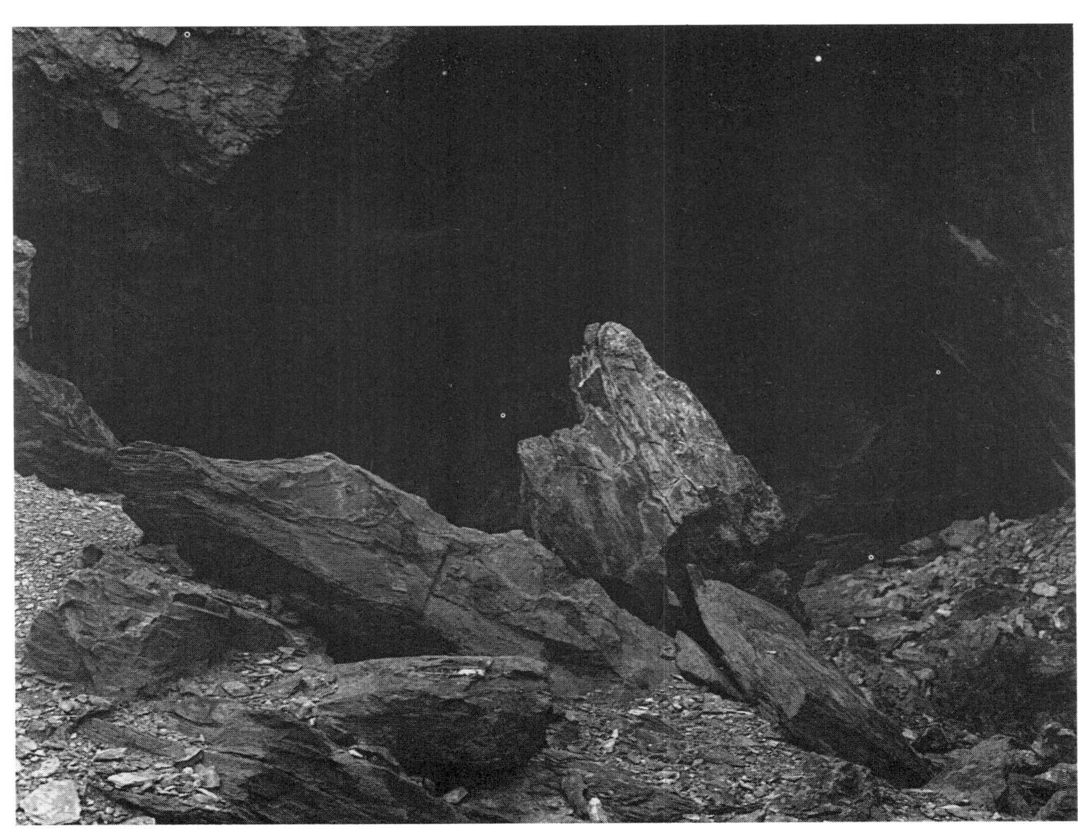

Y TWLL DRWG

The first path winds
and winds in daylight.

If the air allows
I light a candle,
hold it in wet clay

this is the miner's candlestick.

One hand holds the candle
the other holds the ladder

I start to descend.

The ladder leads to a low tunnel
I walk 30 yards towards the east,
then north 15 yards.

I am in Gwaith yr Hwntw Mawr,
a heavy, tiresome place.

I fall down another ladder
                    then another.
I slide through a low narrow opening,
my chin between my knees.

Two ladders come to my hands,
I fall sideways,
multi-coloured rock and clay
                         paent melyn,
                         bluestone.

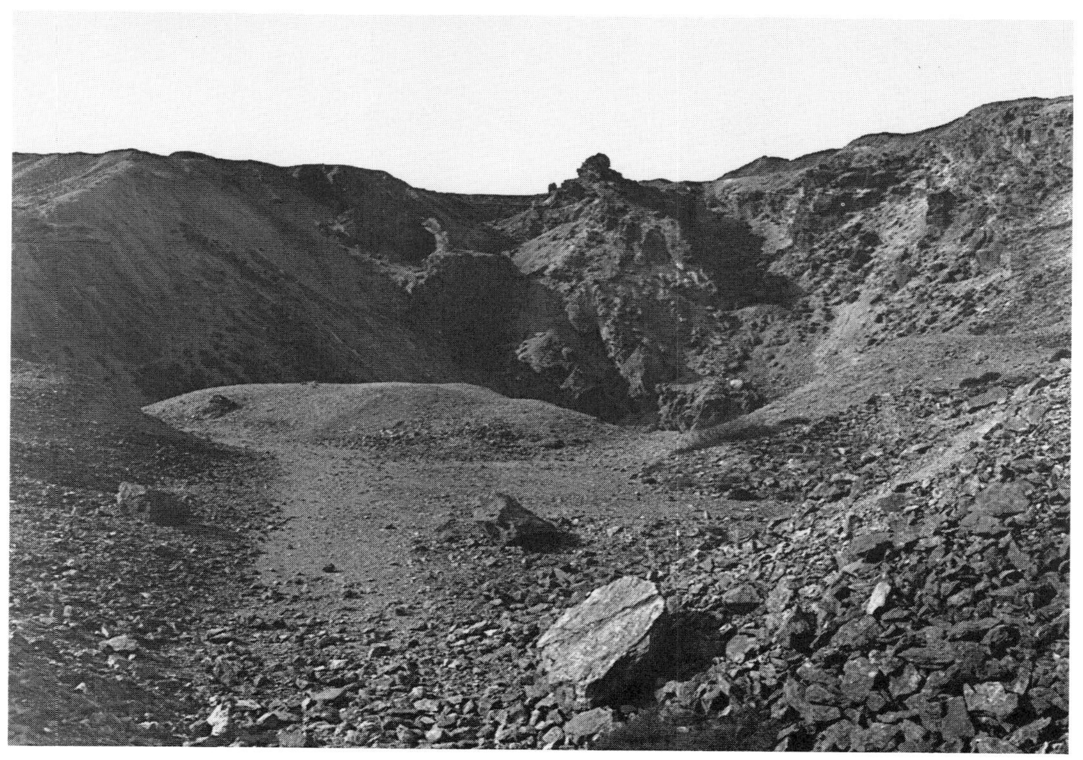

I steep down a muddy path
drag through a nostril-size entrance.
I bend in a half-circle
down to level 30.

This is the first open place I have come to.
                              I must rest.

Cathedrals of sulphur
of green slime.

Boreholes full of water,
the stink of sulphates
and iron.

I move on
in my own light.

Another ladder
then half-slide in mud and water.
This was the hardest path in all the mountain.
I fall to level 44.

Siafft y Garnedd
50 yards down a stone stairway,
I squirm, crawl for half an hour
the shaft whirpools in front.

I survey the lode.

Ladders wait to take me further,
a clumsy ox, I scrabble on the steep face
down to level 70.
I swing on a chain ladder
like a clock's pendulum,
    level 80.

A yellow rope drops me further.

My feet on new rock
freshly cut and fired.
The miners are sinking a new shaft.

My breath is sharp,
the smoke thick as porridge.

Water falls until I soak
from head to foot.

Small springs gush from joints
washing the cheeks of this beautiful rock

this rock of yellow copper veins
this rock of golden wires.

Notes

Y Twll Drwg — The Bad Hole
Gwaith yr Hwntw Mawr — Hwntw Mawr Works
paent melyn — yellow ochre.
survey the lode — evaluate the amount of copper in the rock
Parts of this poem were found in a book called Mynydd Parys *by Owen Griffiths. I translated and adapted it from the Welsh.*

INJIAN CERRIG Y BLEIDDIAU

When Robert Owen was a boy
he could hear the engine
      all day
thumping, thumping
like men's hearts.

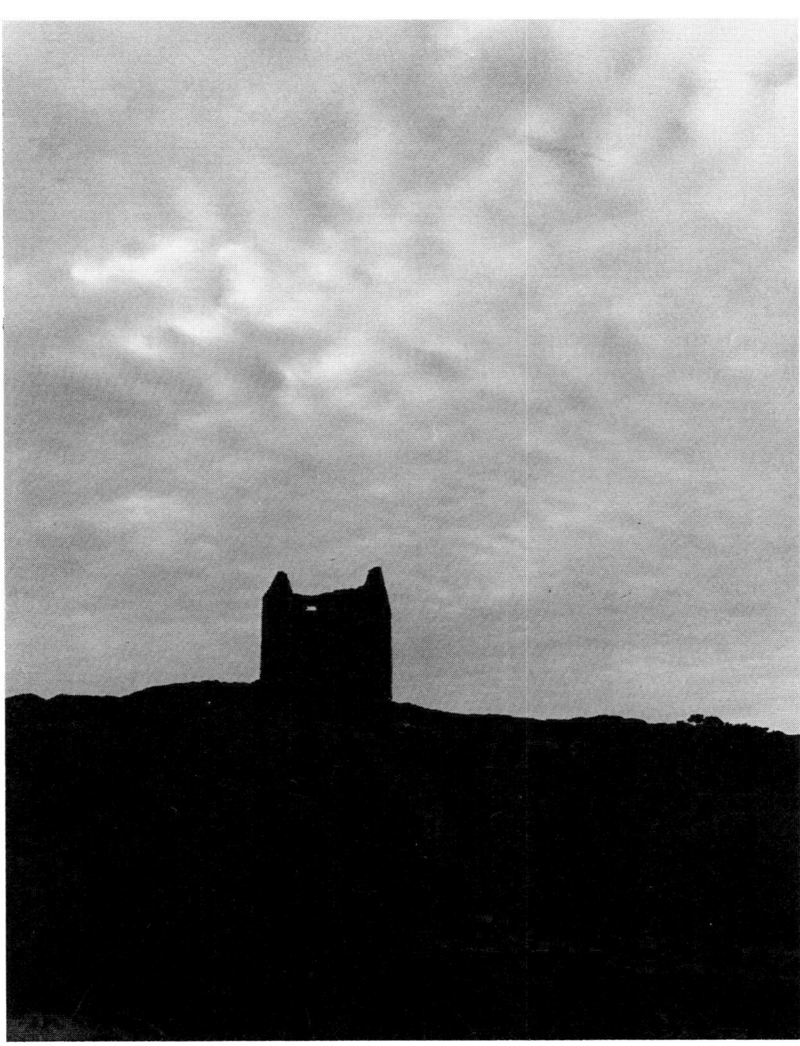

MELIN COPA'R MYNYDD

I walk small vertebrae
                     of stone,
tread a ridge of spoil-tips,
                      the sun red
        in my hand.

The mill stands rotten-toothed
wind cracked stone.

My shadow leaps
                into blue and pink,
                  it stands
              a hole in light.

I am between yellow and sky,
in the sea's ring
in the call of ravens.

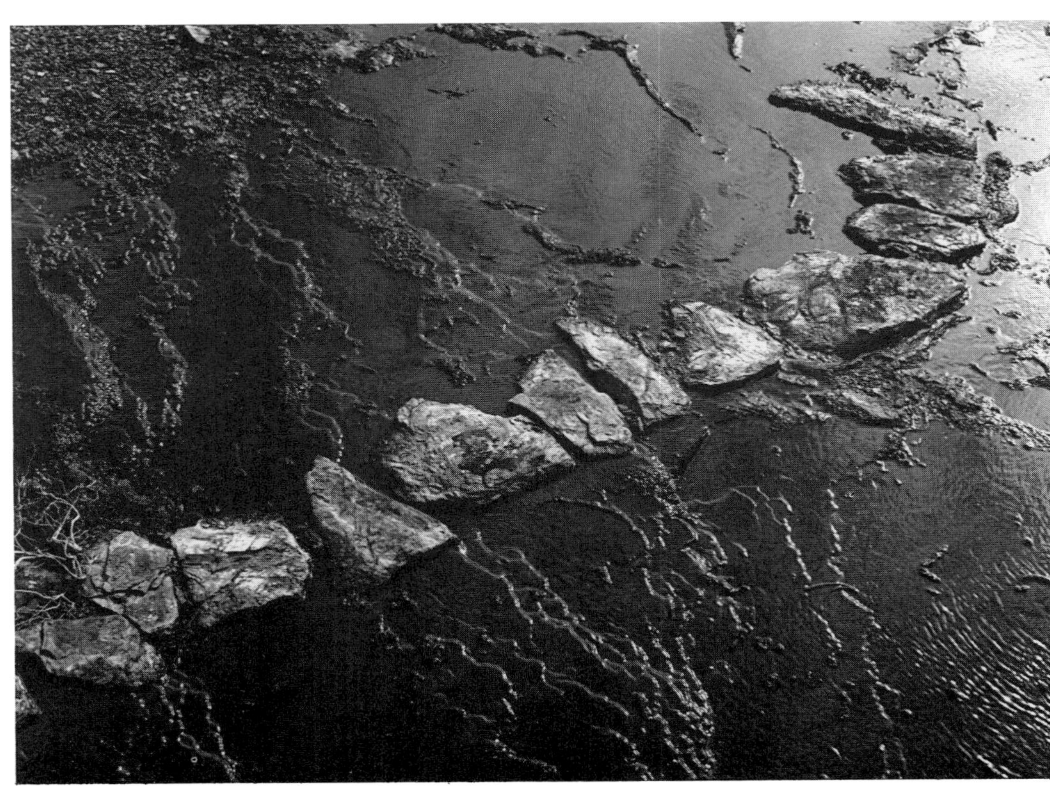

RUBBISH

Fridges gape
       the baked heat
       of summer

a broken protractor
       shatters angles
       on stone

car bodies
       glacier
       to the acid lake.

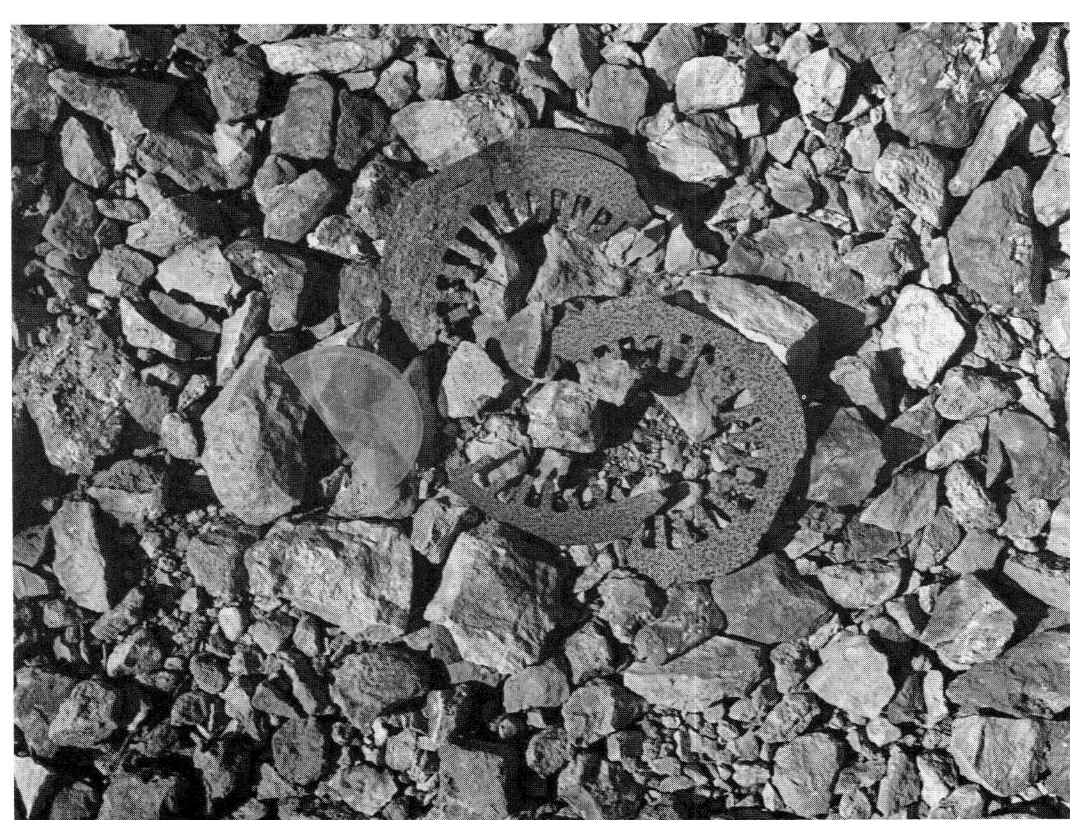

DYFFRYN COCH

There are white flames burning
in Dyffryn Coch,
cotton-grass beards the lake,
bog-land dry as biscuit.

Heather and gorse
grows on metal and rubber,
the ground freckled
burnt sulphur.

In the evening
the mountain settles its stone skirt,
sighs,
in the swift-scream light.

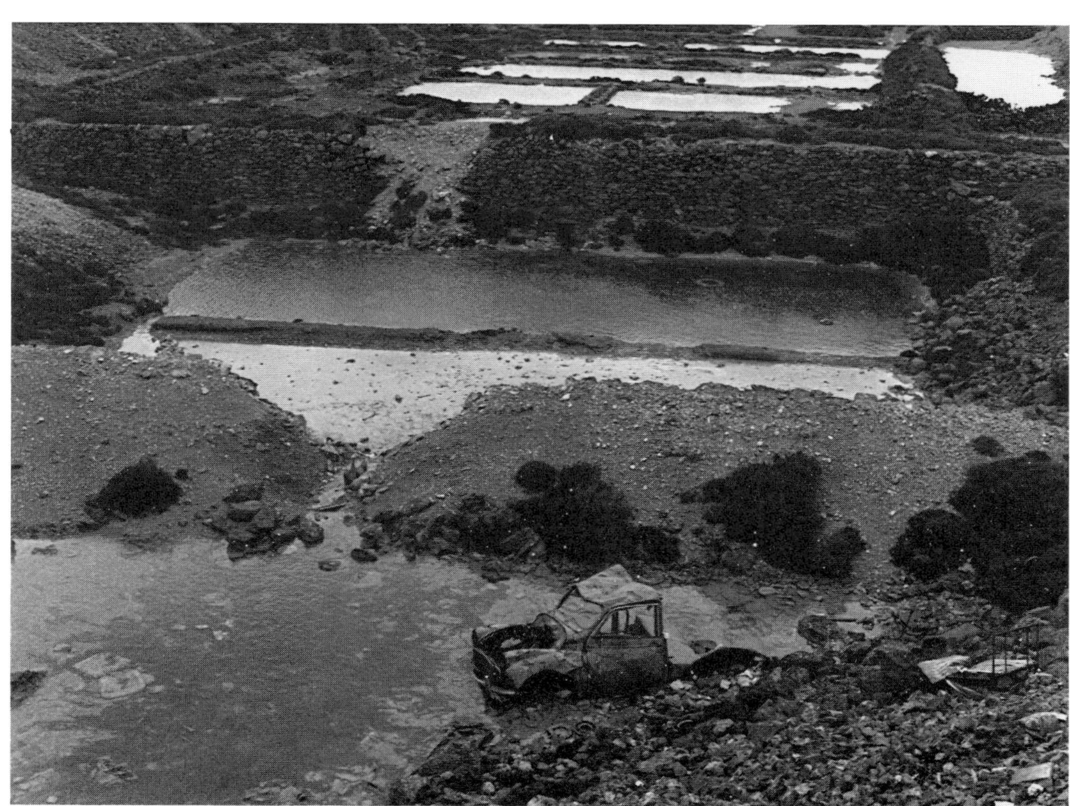

OWAIN HUGHES, PRECIPITATE WORKER (1896–1985)

When I started work in the mountain
I was 17 years old. I worked on level 45 fathoms
I never could go down further, me that is.
I used to start at 6 and finish at 5,
that was when I started, in 1913.

I worked the water you know,
scrap iron and that, copper precipitate and paint.
I pumped water into the mountain
I went to the old workings where the water could not reach.
With water in pipes I sprayed the rock
to strengthen precipitate.

They got ochre from the pools at Pentrefelin, you know,
I remember the paintworks in Amlwch,
I remember it standing, you know, on its feet
a huge chimney on it.

With water I went down the shafts
ropes and footwires down,
one ladder then another,
footwires they called them.
There were 800 men underground,
my grandmother told me that,
800 down below.

My dad was an engine driver,
pumped water to relieve the engines
all his life.
I pumped water out all day,
all wet when I had been down the level.

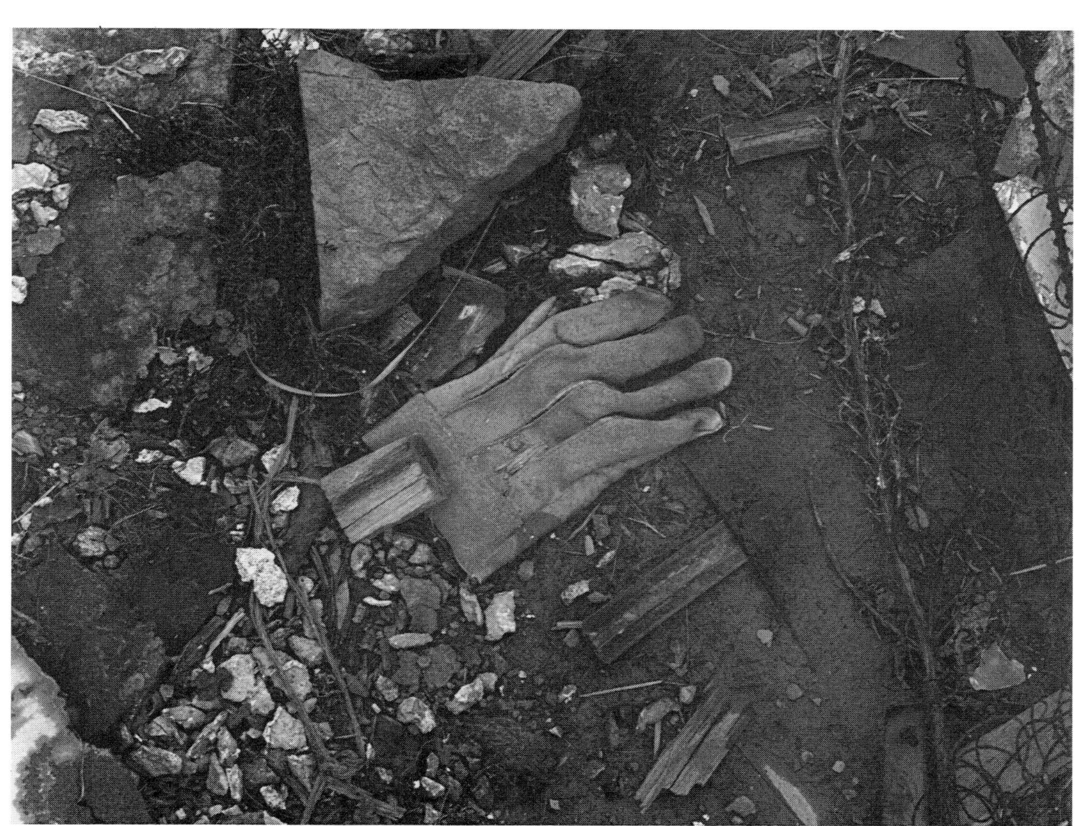

When I was 20, the war,
the First World War.
We were working the garreglas,
blende ore in english.
I was the youngest there, as I know it.

Too many went away to fight,
boys from Llanfechell, Llaneilian,
I was sent to Ypres.

Well, there was nothing important here, you know,
just poor;
poor wages.

Owain Huges lived all his life in Cerrigman near Amlwch, at the foot
of Mynydd Parys. I interviewed him a few years before his death. I
translated from Welsh.

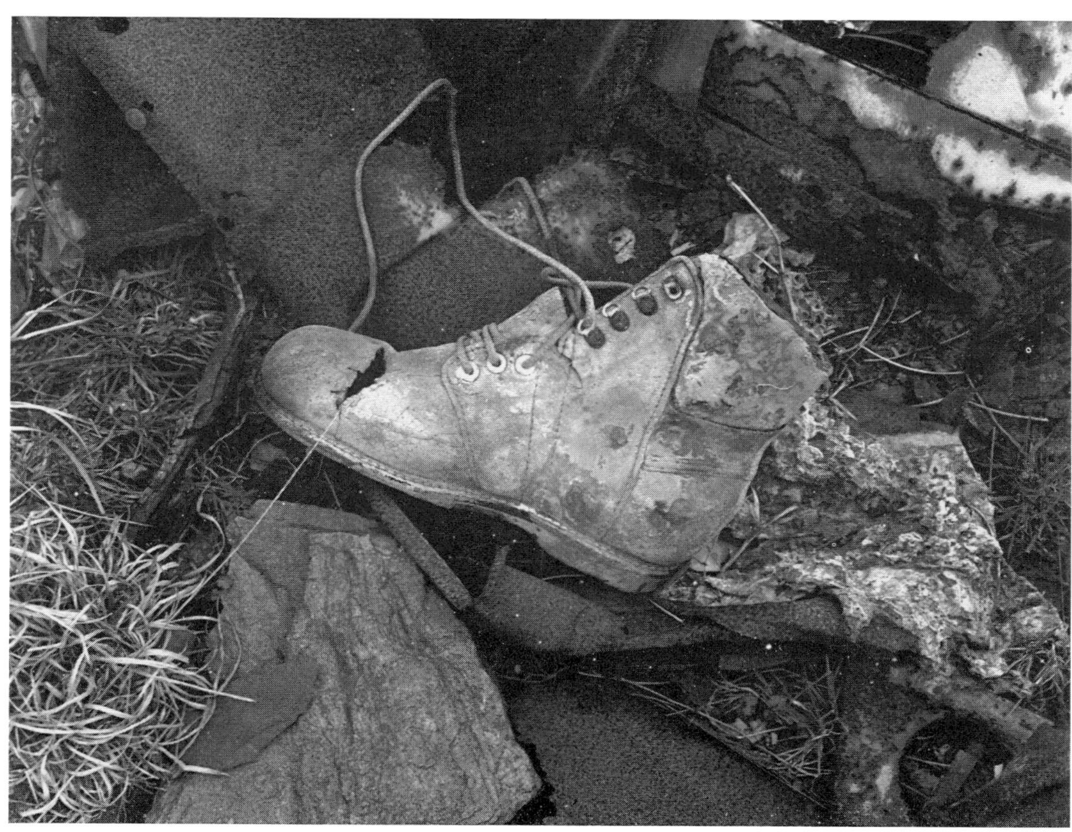

SLEDGING

We made sledges from car bonnets,
ford anglias or a wide zephyr,
so that we could fit four on.
From the top of the purple-slime
near the Mona Yard
we fireworked our way down
rocks cracking underneath.

Still I see the glints of bonnets,
feel the warmth of metal in summer sun,
hear our voices circle the open cast.

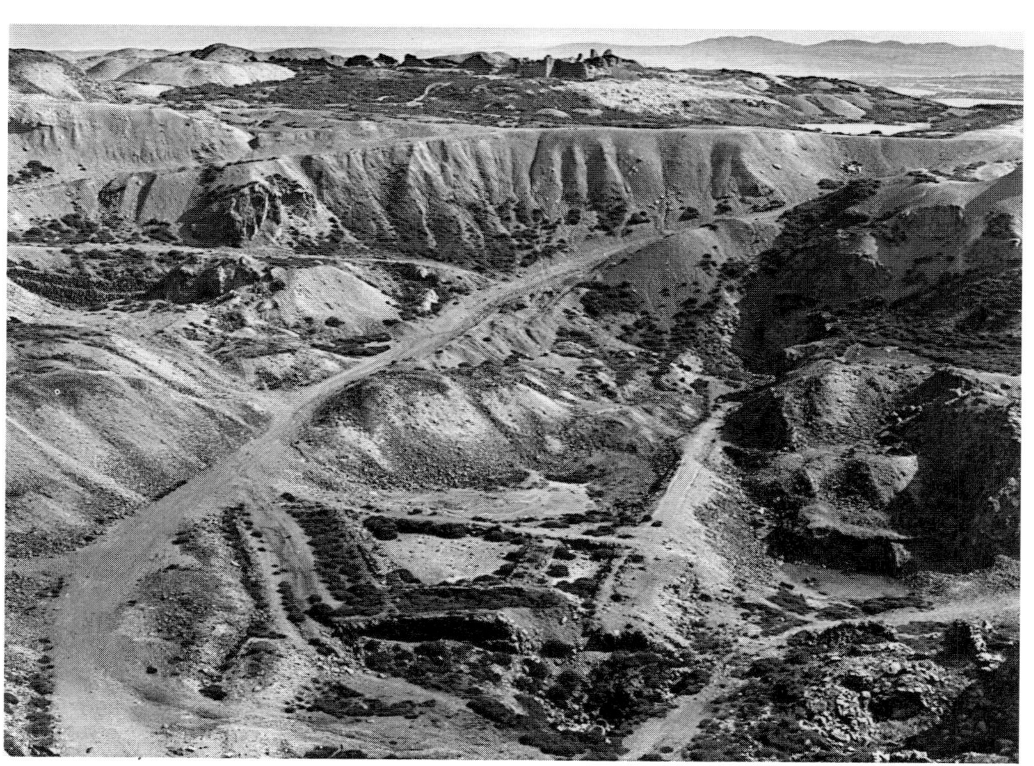

RECLAMATION

The council are making paths for the public,
blue stones and gleaming gates,
yellow arrows that point the way.
Two shafts have been filled,
the small pouting one
the water-dark one.
An air-vent is ruined by JCBs.
Roads and cartways are blocked.

The mountain is now safe,
except for its colour --
the yellow that blinds,
the blue after rain,
the blood red of sunset.

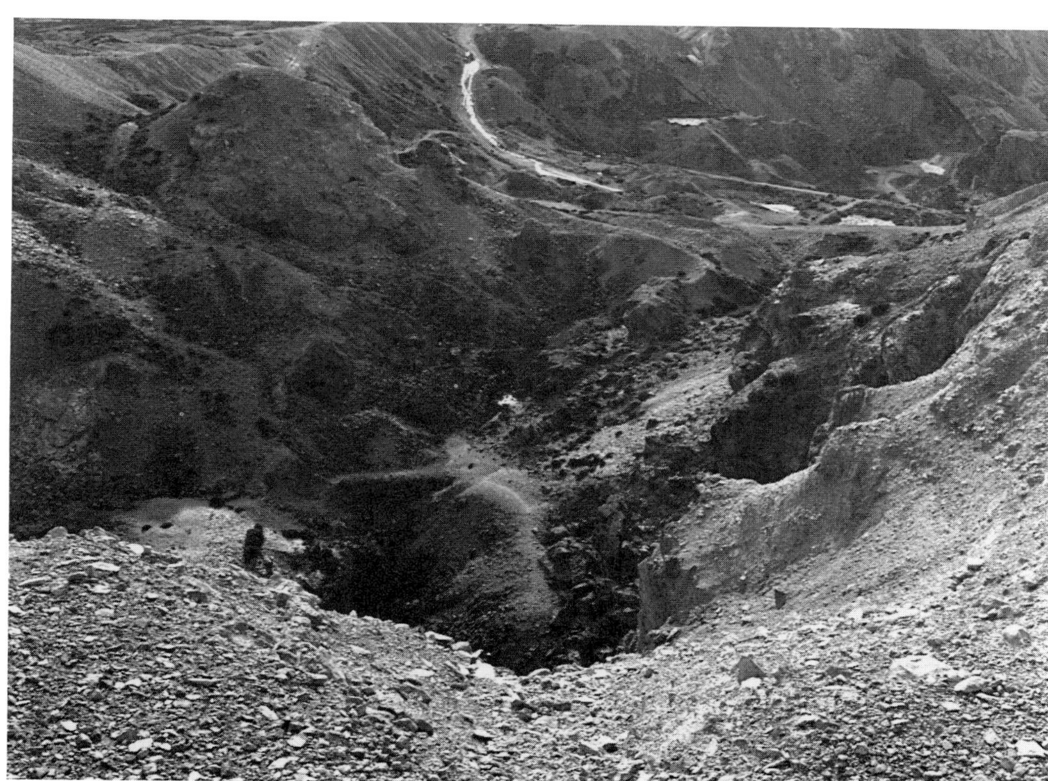

ACKNOWLEDGEMENTS

Diolch yn fawr i Ceri ac Alan am rhoi lle i fi fyw, a diolch i phawb sydd wedi rhoi cymorth i mi. — G.P.

Thank you to GP for access and JS (now JM!) for much tolerance and support. Also, thanks to Paul Hill, John Blakemore and Tom Cooper for their encouragement and advice. — S.M.